Soups & Breads

Mug 'Ems make great gifts for your family and friends. Use the recipes in this book to assemble your homemade gift. Place the ingredients in a ziplock or food-safe bag and set the sealed bag in a decorative mug. Each recipe includes gift tags for your convenience — just cut them out, fold and personalize. Attach the personalized tag to the mug and decorate with ribbon, fabric and raffia.

When making these homemade gifts, use mugs that hold a volume of at least 1½ cups. For safety reasons, it is important that you do not give your gift in a metal or plastic mug.

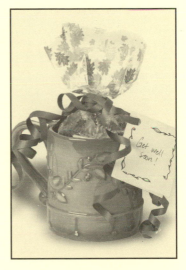

Printed in the United States of America
by G&R Publishing Co.

Distributed By:

507 Industrial Street
Waverly, IA 50677

ISBN-13: 978-1-56383-200-0
ISBN-10: 1-56383-200-3
Item #3772

Split Pea Soup Mix

¼ C. green split peas
½ tsp. dried onion flakes
½ tsp. crumbled bay leaf
Pinch of pepper
2 tsp. dried celery flakes
1 T. real bacon bits
1 tsp. chicken bouillon

In a small bowl, combine green split peas, dried onion flakes, crumbled bay leaf, pepper, dried celery flakes, bacon bits and chicken bouillon. Mix well and place in a small ziplock bag and seal. Place sealed bag in mug. Make sure the mug holds a volume of at least 1½ cups.

Decorate mug and attach a gift tag with the directions on how to prepare the soup.

Gift Tag Directions:
Split Pea Soup

Split Pea Soup Mix
1 C. plus 2 T. water

Preheat oven to 325°. Place Split Pea Soup Mix from bag in mug. In small saucepan, place water. Bring water to a simmer and pour over ingredients in mug. Mix well and cover with aluminum foil. Bake in oven for 55 to 60 minutes, stirring after 30 minutes of baking time. As needed, add a few tablespoons of water during baking to ensure mug stays full. Enjoy!

Split Pea Soup

Split Pea Soup Mix
1 C. plus 2 T. water

Preheat oven to 325°. Place Split Pea Soup Mix from bag in mug. In small saucepan, place water. Bring water to a simmer and pour over ingredients in mug. Mix well and cover with aluminum foil. Bake in oven for 55 to 60 minutes, stirring after 30 minutes of baking time. As needed, add a few tablespoons of water during baking to ensure mug stays full. Enjoy!

Split Pea Soup

Split Pea Soup Mix
1 C. plus 2 T. water

Preheat oven to 325°. Place Split Pea Soup Mix from bag in mug. In small saucepan, place water. Bring water to a simmer and pour over ingredients in mug. Mix well and cover with aluminum foil. Bake in oven for 55 to 60 minutes, stirring after 30 minutes of baking time. As needed, add a few tablespoons of water during baking to ensure mug stays full. Enjoy!

You've
Been
Mugged!

You've
Been
Mugged!

MUG'EMS
by
CQ Products
www.cqproducts.com

MUG'EMS
by
CQ Products
www.cqproducts.com

Split Pea Soup

Split Pea Soup Mix
1 C. plus 2 T. water

Preheat oven to 325°. Place Split Pea Soup Mix from bag in mug. In small saucepan, place water. Bring water to a simmer and pour over ingredients in mug. Mix well and cover with aluminum foil. Bake in oven for 55 to 60 minutes, stirring after 30 minutes of baking time. As needed, add a few tablespoons of water during baking to ensure mug stays full. Enjoy!

Split Pea Soup

Split Pea Soup Mix
1 C. plus 2 T. water

Preheat oven to 325°. Place Split Pea Soup Mix from bag in mug. In small saucepan, place water. Bring water to a simmer and pour over ingredients in mug. Mix well and cover with aluminum foil. Bake in oven for 55 to 60 minutes, stirring after 30 minutes of baking time. As needed, add a few tablespoons of water during baking to ensure mug stays full. Enjoy!

fold

You've
Been
Mugged!

MUG'EMS
by
CQ Products
www.cqproducts.com

You've
Been
Mugged!

MUG'EMS
by
CQ Products
www.cqproducts.com

Cream of Potato Soup Mix

5½ T. potato flakes
½ tsp. dillweed
Pinch of pepper
½ tsp. salt
½ tsp. dried onion flakes
1 T. Knorr classic white sauce mix

In a small bowl, combine potato flakes, dillweed, pepper, salt, dried onion flakes and white sauce mix. Mix well and place in a small ziplock bag and seal. Place sealed bag in a mug. Make sure the mug holds a volume of at least 1½ cups.

Decorate mug and attach a gift tag with the directions on how to prepare the soup.

Gift Tag Directions:
Cream of Potato Soup

Cream of Potato Soup Mix
1¼ C. water
1 T. butter

Place Cream of Potato Soup Mix from bag in mug. In a small saucepan over medium heat, place water and butter. Mix well and bring to a boil. Pour heated butter mixture over ingredients in mug. Mix well, cover and let sit for 5 minutes. If desired, top with shredded Cheddar cheese, sour cream or soda crackers. Enjoy!

Cream of
Potato Soup

Cream of Potato Soup Mix
1¼ C. water
1 T. butter

   Place Cream of Potato Soup Mix from bag in mug. In a small saucepan over medium heat, place water and butter. Mix well and bring to a boil. Pour heated butter mixture over ingredients in mug. Mix well, cover and let sit for 5 minutes. If desired, top with shredded Cheddar cheese, sour cream or soda crackers. Enjoy!

Cream of
Potato Soup

Cream of Potato Soup Mix
1¼ C. water
1 T. butter

   Place Cream of Potato Soup Mix from bag in mug. In a small saucepan over medium heat, place water and butter. Mix well and bring to a boil. Pour heated butter mixture over ingredients in mug. Mix well, cover and let sit for 5 minutes. If desired, top with shredded Cheddar cheese, sour cream or soda crackers. Enjoy!

fold

You've
Been
Mugged!

MUG'EMS
by
CQ Products
www.cqproducts.com

You've
Been
Mugged!

MUG'EMS
by
CQ Products
www.cqproducts.com

Cream of
Potato Soup

Cream of Potato Soup Mix
1¼ C. water
1 T. butter

Place Cream of Potato Soup Mix from bag in mug. In a small saucepan over medium heat, place water and butter. Mix well and bring to a boil. Pour heated butter mixture over ingredients in mug. Mix well, cover and let sit for 5 minutes. If desired, top with shredded Cheddar cheese, sour cream or soda crackers. Enjoy!

Cream of
Potato Soup

Cream of Potato Soup Mix
1¼ C. water
1 T. butter

Place Cream of Potato Soup Mix from bag in mug. In a small saucepan over medium heat, place water and butter. Mix well and bring to a boil. Pour heated butter mixture over ingredients in mug. Mix well, cover and let sit for 5 minutes. If desired, top with shredded Cheddar cheese, sour cream or soda crackers. Enjoy!

fold

You've
Been
Mugged!

MUG'EMS
by
CQ Products
www.cqproducts.com

You've
Been
Mugged!

MUG'EMS
by
CQ Products
www.cqproducts.com

Old Fashioned Corn Bread Mix

3 T. flour
3 T. cornmeal
2 tsp. sugar
¾ tsp. baking powder
⅛ tsp. salt

In a small bowl, combine flour, cornmeal, sugar, baking powder and salt. Mix well and place in small ziplock bag and seal. Place sealed bag in a mug. Make sure the mug holds a volume of at least 1½ cups.

Decorate mug and attach a gift tag with the directions on how to prepare the bread.

Gift Tag Directions:
Old Fashioned Corn Bread

Old Fashioned Corn Bread Mix
3 T. buttermilk or milk
1 small egg
1 T. butter

Preheat oven to 375°. Place Old Fashioned Corn Bread Mix from bag in a small bowl. Add buttermilk, egg and butter. Beat until smooth and pour into lightly greased mug. Bake in oven for 18 to 22 minutes. Enjoy!

Old Fashioned
Corn Bread

Old Fashioned Corn
   Bread Mix
3 T. buttermilk or milk
1 small egg
1 T. butter

Preheat oven to 375°. Place Old Fashioned Corn Bread Mix from bag in a small bowl. Add buttermilk, egg and butter. Beat until smooth and pour into lightly greased mug. Bake in oven for 18 to 22 minutes. Enjoy!

Old Fashioned
Corn Bread

Old Fashioned Corn
   Mix Bread
3 T. buttermilk or milk
1 small egg
1 T. butter

Preheat oven to 375°. Place Old Fashioned Corn Bread Mix from bag in a small bowl. Add buttermilk, egg and butter. Beat until smooth and pour into lightly greased mug. Bake in oven for 18 to 22 minutes. Enjoy!

You've
Been
Mugged!

MUG'EMS
by
CQ Products
www.cqproducts.com

You've
Been
Mugged!

MUG'EMS
by
CQ Products
www.cqproducts.com

← fold →

Old Fashioned
Corn Bread

Old Fashioned Corn
Mix Bread
3 T. buttermilk or milk
1 small egg
1 T. butter

Preheat oven to 375°. Place Old Fashioned Corn Bread Mix from bag in a small bowl. Add buttermilk, egg and butter. Beat until smooth and pour into lightly greased mug. Bake in oven for 18 to 22 minutes. Enjoy!

Old Fashioned
Corn Bread

Old Fashioned Corn
Mix Bread
3 T. buttermilk or milk
1 small egg
1 T. butter

Preheat oven to 375°. Place Old Fashioned Corn Bread Mix from bag in a small bowl. Add buttermilk, egg and butter. Beat until smooth and pour into lightly greased mug. Bake in oven for 18 to 22 minutes. Enjoy!

← fold →

You've
Been
Mugged!

You've
Been
Mugged!

MUG'EMS
by
CQ Products
www.cqproducts.com

MUG'EMS
by
CQ Products
www.cqproducts.com

Chicken & Rice Soup Mix

2 T. instant rice
1½ tsp. chicken bouillon
¼ tsp. dried onion flakes
Pinch of pepper
1 tsp. dried parsley flakes
1 tsp. dried celery flakes
1 (4½ oz.) can chunk chicken, drained

In a small bowl, combine instant rice, chicken bouillon, dried onion flakes, pepper, dried parsley flakes and dried celery flakes. Mix well and place in small ziplock bag and seal. Place sealed bag in a mug. Make sure the mug holds a volume of at least 1½ cups.

Decorate mug and attach a gift tag with the directions on how to prepare the soup.

Gift Tag Directions:
Chicken & Rice Soup

Chicken & Rice Soup Mix
¾ C. water

Place Chicken & Rice Soup Mix from bag in mug. In small saucepan over medium heat, place water. Bring water to a boil and pour over ingredients in mug. Cover and let sit for 5 minutes. Add drained chicken from can to ingredients in mug. Mix well and heat in microwave for 1 to 2 minutes. Enjoy!

Chicken & Rice Soup

Chicken & Rice Soup Mix
¾ C. water

Place Chicken & Rice Soup Mix from bag in mug. In small saucepan over medium heat, place water. Bring water to a boil and pour over ingredients in mug. Cover and let sit for 5 minutes. Add drained chicken from can to ingredients in mug. Mix well and heat in microwave for 1 to 2 minutes. Enjoy!

Chicken & Rice Soup

Chicken & Rice Soup Mix
¾ C. water

Place Chicken & Rice Soup Mix from bag in mug. In small saucepan over medium heat, place water. Bring water to a boil and pour over ingredients in mug. Cover and let sit for 5 minutes. Add drained chicken from can to ingredients in mug. Mix well and heat in microwave for 1 to 2 minutes. Enjoy!

← fold →

You've
Been
Mugged!

You've
Been
Mugged!

MUG'EMS
by
CQ Products
www.cqproducts.com

MUG'EMS
by
CQ Products
www.cqproducts.com

Chicken &
Rice Soup

Chicken & Rice Soup Mix
¾ C. water

Place Chicken & Rice Soup Mix from bag in mug. In small saucepan over medium heat, place water. Bring water to a boil and pour over ingredients in mug. Cover and let sit for 5 minutes. Add drained chicken from can to ingredients In mug. Mix well and heat in microwave for 1 to 2 minutes. Enjoy!

Chicken &
Rice Soup

Chicken & Rice Soup Mix
¾ C. water

Place Chicken & Rice Soup Mix from bag in mug. In small saucepan over medium heat, place water. Bring water to a boil and pour over ingredients in mug. Cover and let sit for 5 minutes. Add drained chicken from can to ingredients in mug. Mix well and heat in microwave for 1 to 2 minutes. Enjoy!

← fold →

You've
Been
Mugged!

You've
Been
Mugged!

MUG'EMS
by
Products
www.cqproducts.com

MUG'EMS
by
Products
www.cqproducts.com

Beef & Barley Stew Mix

3 T. brown lentils
1 T. quick cooking barley
2 tsp. beef bouillon
1 tsp. dried celery flakes
½ tsp. dried onion flakes

In a small bowl, combine brown lentils, barley, beef bouillon, dried celery flakes and onion. Mix well and place in small ziplock bag and seal. Place sealed bag in a mug. Make sure the mug holds a volume of at least 1½ cups.

Decorate mug and attach a gift tag with the directions on how to prepare the stew.

Gift Tag Directions:
Beef & Barley Stew

Beef & Barley Stew Mix
1 C. water
1 tsp. olive oil

Preheat oven to 325°. Place Beef & Barley Stew Mix from bag in mug. In small saucepan over medium heat, combine water and olive oil. Bring to a simmer and pour over ingredients in mug. Loosely cover mug with a small piece of aluminum foil. Bake in oven for 35 to 40 minutes. As needed, add a few tablespoons of water during baking to ensure mug stays full. Enjoy!

Beef &
Barley Stew

Beef & Barley Stew Mix
1 C. water
1 tsp. olive oil

Preheat oven to 325°. Place Beef & Barley Stew Mix from bag in mug. In small saucepan over medium heat, combine water and olive oil. Bring to a simmer and pour over ingredients in mug. Loosely cover mug with a small piece of aluminum foil. Bake in oven for 35 to 40 minutes. As needed, add a few tablespoons of water during baking to ensure mug stays full. Enjoy!

Beef &
Barley Stew

Beef & Barley Stew Mix
1 C. water
1 tsp. olive oil

Preheat oven to 325°. Place Beef & Barley Stew Mix from bag in mug. In small saucepan over medium heat, combine water and olive oil. Bring to a simmer and pour over ingredients in mug. Loosely cover mug with a small piece of aluminum foil. Bake in oven for 35 to 40 minutes. As needed, add a few tablespoons of water during baking to ensure mug stays full. Enjoy!

← fold →

You've
Been
Mugged!

MUG'EMS
by
CQ Products
www.cqproducts.com

You've
Been
Mugged!

MUG'EMS
by
CQ Products
www.cqproducts.com

Beef &
Barley Stew

Beef & Barley Stew Mix
1 C. water
1 tsp. olive oil

Preheat oven to 325°. Place Beef & Barley Stew Mix from bag in mug. In small saucepan over medium heat, combine water and olive oil. Bring to a simmer and pour over ingredients in mug. Loosely cover mug with a small piece of aluminum foil. Bake in oven for 35 to 40 minutes. As needed, add a few tablespoons of water during baking to ensure mug stays full. Enjoy!

Beef &
Barley Stew

Beef & Barley Stew Mix
1 C. water
1 tsp. olive oil

Preheat oven to 325°. Place Beef & Barley Stew Mix from bag in mug. In small saucepan over medium heat, combine water and olive oil. Bring to a simmer and pour over ingredients in mug. Loosely cover mug with a small piece of aluminum foil. Bake in oven for 35 to 40 minutes. As needed, add a few tablespoons of water during baking to ensure mug stays full. Enjoy!

← fold →

You've
Been
Mugged!

You've
Been
Mugged!

MUG'EMS
by
CQ Products
www.cqproducts.com

MUG'EMS
by
CQ Products
www.cqproducts.com

Country Raisin Bread Mix

1½ T. raisins
1½ T. sugar
½ tsp. baking powder
¼ tsp. cinnamon
¼ tsp. baking soda
Pinch of salt
Pinch of nutmeg
⅓ C. flour

In a small bowl, combine raisins, sugar, baking powder, cinnamon, baking soda, salt, nutmeg and flour. Mix well and place in a small ziplock bag and seal. Place sealed bag in a mug. Make sure the mug holds a volume of at least 1½ cups.

Decorate mug and attach a gift tag with the directions on how to prepare the bread.

Gift Tag Directions:
Country Raisin Bread

Country Raisin Bread Mix
1½ T. milk
1 egg, beaten
1 T. butter or margarine, melted

Preheat oven to 350°. Place Country Raisin Bread Mix from bag in mug. Add milk and half of the beaten egg and mix well. Add melted butter and stir for 1 minute. Pour batter into lightly greased mug. Bake in oven for 20 to 25 minutes. Enjoy!

Country Raisin Bread

Country Raisin Bread Mix
1½ T. milk
1 egg, beaten
1 T. butter or margarine,
   melted

   Preheat oven to 350°. Place Country Raisin Bread Mix from bag in mug. Add milk and half of the beaten egg and mix well. Add melted butter and stir for 1 minute. Pour batter into lightly greased mug. Bake in oven for 20 to 25 minutes. Enjoy!

Country Raisin Bread

Country Raisin Bread Mix
1½ T. milk
1 egg, beaten
1 T. butter or margarine,
   melted

   Preheat oven to 350°. Place Country Raisin Bread Mix from bag in mug. Add milk and half of the beaten egg and mix well. Add melted butter and stir for 1 minute. Pour batter into lightly greased mug. Bake in oven for 20 to 25 minutes. Enjoy!

You've
Been
Mugged!

MUG'EMS
by
CQ Products
www.cqproducts.com

You've
Been
Mugged!

MUG'EMS
by
CQ Products
www.cqproducts.com

← fold →

Country Raisin Bread

Country Raisin Bread Mix
1½ T. milk
1 egg, beaten
1 T. butter or margarine,
   melted

Preheat oven to 350°. Place Country Raisin Bread Mix from bag in mug. Add milk and half of the beaten egg and mix well. Add melted butter and stir for 1 minute. Pour batter into lightly greased mug. Bake in oven for 20 to 25 minutes. Enjoy!

Country Raisin Bread

Country Raisin Bread Mix
1½ T. milk
1 egg, beaten
1 T. butter or margarine,
   melted

Preheat oven to 350°. Place Country Raisin Bread Mix from bag in mug. Add milk and half of the beaten egg and mix well. Add melted butter and stir for 1 minute. Pour batter into lightly greased mug. Bake in oven for 20 to 25 minutes. Enjoy!

You've
Been
Mugged!

MUG'EMS
by
CQ Products
www.cqproducts.com

You've
Been
Mugged!

MUG'EMS
by
CQ Products
www.cqproducts.com

Coffee Cake Mix

⅓ C. plus 1 T. flour,
    divided
2 T. sugar
½ tsp. baking powder
¼ tsp. cinnamon
⅛ tsp. baking soda

Pinch of salt
Pinch of nutmeg
Pinch of ground cloves
1½ T. brown sugar
2 T. finely chopped
    nuts

In a small bowl, combine ⅓ cup flour, sugar, baking powder, cinnamon, baking soda, salt, nutmeg and ground cloves. Mix well and place in small ziplock bag and seal. Place sealed bag in mug. Make sure the mug holds a volume of at least 1½ cups. In a separate ziplock bag, place remaining 1 tablespoon flour, brown sugar and chopped nuts. Place bag inside mug with other bag.

Decorate mug and attach a gift tag with the directions on how to prepare the coffee cake.

Gift Tag Directions:
Coffee Cake

Coffee Cake Mix
3 T. buttermilk
1½ T. butter or margarine, melted, divided
1 egg, beaten

Preheat oven to 350°. In small bowl, place contents of bag containing sugar. Add buttermilk, 1 tablespoon melted butter and half of the beaten egg. Mix well and pour into lightly greased mug. In a small bowl, combine contents of remaining bag with remaining ½ tablespoon melted butter. Mix until small crumbs form. Sprinkle crumb topping over batter in mug. Bake in oven for 20 to 25 minutes. Enjoy!

Coffee Cake

Coffee Cake Mix
3 T. buttermilk
1½ T. butter or margarine,
    melted, divided
1 egg, beaten

Preheat oven to 350°. In small bowl, place contents of bag containing sugar. Add buttermilk, 1 tablespoon melted butter and half of the beaten egg. Mix well and pour into lightly greased mug. In a small bowl, combine contents of remaining bag with remaining ½ tablespoon melted butter. Mix until small crumbs form. Sprinkle crumb topping over batter in mug. Bake in oven for 20 to 25 minutes. Enjoy!

Coffee Cake

Coffee Cake Mix
3 T. buttermilk
1½ T. butter or margarine,
    melted, divided
1 egg, beaten

Preheat oven to 350°. In small bowl, place contents of bag containing sugar. Add buttermilk, 1 tablespoon melted butter and half of the beaten egg. Mix well and pour into lightly greased mug. In a small bowl, combine contents of remaining bag with remaining ½ tablespoon melted butter. Mix until small crumbs form. Sprinkle crumb topping over batter in mug. Bake in oven for 20 to 25 minutes. Enjoy!

← fold →

You've
Been
Mugged!

You've
Been
Mugged!

MUG'EMS
by
CQ Products
www.cqproducts.com

MUG'EMS
by
CQ Products
www.cqproducts.com

Coffee Cake

Coffee Cake Mix
3 T. buttermilk
1½ T. butter or margarine,
  melted, divided
1 egg, beaten

Preheat oven to 350°. In small bowl, place contents of bag containing sugar. Add buttermilk, 1 tablespoon melted butter and half of the beaten egg. Mix well and pour into lightly greased mug. In a small bowl, combine contents of remaining bag with remaining ½ tablespoon melted butter. Mix until small crumbs form. Sprinkle crumb topping over batter in mug. Bake in oven for 20 to 25 minutes. Enjoy!

Coffee Cake

Coffee Cake Mix
3 T. buttermilk
1½ T. butter or margarine,
  melted, divided
1 egg, beaten

Preheat oven to 350°. In small bowl, place contents of bag containing sugar. Add buttermilk, 1 tablespoon melted butter and half of the beaten egg. Mix well and pour into lightly greased mug. In a small bowl, combine contents of remaining bag with remaining ½ tablespoon melted butter. Mix until small crumbs form. Sprinkle crumb topping over batter in mug. Bake in oven for 20 to 25 minutes. Enjoy!

← fold →

You've
Been
Mugged!

You've
Been
Mugged!

MUG'EMS
by
CQ Products
www.cqproducts.com

MUG'EMS
by
CQ Products
www.cqproducts.com

Herbed Soda Bread Mix

⅓ C. flour
½ tsp. sugar
¾ tsp. baking soda
⅛ tsp. salt
½ tsp. dried parsley flakes
½ tsp. dillweed
½ tsp. dried basil

In a small bowl, combine flour, sugar, baking soda, salt, dried parsley flakes, dillweed and dried basil. Mix well and place in a small ziplock bag and seal. Place sealed bag in a mug. Make sure the mug holds a volume of at least 1½ cups.

Decorate mug and attach a gift tag with the directions on how to prepare the bread.

Gift Tag Directions:
Herbed Soda Bread

Herbed Soda Bread Mix
2 T. buttermilk
1 T. butter or margarine, melted
1 egg, beaten

Preheat oven to 350°. In a small mixing bowl, combine Herbed Soda Bread Mix from bag with buttermilk, melted butter and half of the beaten egg. Pour batter into lightly greased mug. Bake in oven for 20 to 25 minutes. Enjoy!

Herbed
Soda Bread

Herbed Soda Bread Mix
2 T. buttermilk
1 T. butter or margarine,
   melted
1 egg, beaten

   Preheat oven to 350°. In a small mixing bowl, combine Herbed Soda Bread Mix from bag with buttermilk, melted butter and half of the beaten egg. Pour batter into lightly greased mug. Bake in oven for 20 to 25 minutes. Enjoy!

Herbed
Soda Bread

Herbed Soda Bread Mix
2 T. buttermilk
1 T. butter or margarine,
   melted
1 egg, beaten

   Preheat oven to 350°. In a small mixing bowl, combine Herbed Soda Bread Mix from bag with buttermilk, melted butter and half of the beaten egg. Pour batter into lightly greased mug. Bake in oven for 20 to 25 minutes. Enjoy!

You've
Been
Mugged!

MUG'EMS
by
CQ Products
www.cqproducts.com

You've
Been
Mugged!

MUG'EMS
by
CQ Products
www.cqproducts.com

← fold →

Herbed
Soda Bread

Herbed Soda Bread Mix
2 T. buttermilk
1 T. butter or margarine,
   melted
1 egg, beaten

   Preheat oven to 350°. In a small mixing bowl, combine Herbed Soda Bread Mix from bag with buttermilk, melted butter and half of the beaten egg. Pour batter into lightly greased mug. Bake in oven for 20 to 25 minutes. Enjoy!

Herbed
Soda Bread

Herbed Soda Bread Mix
2 T. buttermilk
1 T. butter or margarine,
   melted
1 egg, beaten

   Preheat oven to 350°. In a small mixing bowl, combine Herbed Soda Bread Mix from bag with buttermilk, melted butter and half of the beaten egg. Pour batter into lightly greased mug. Bake in oven for 20 to 25 minutes. Enjoy!

← fold →

You've
Been
Mugged!

MUG'EMS
by
CQ Products
www.cqproducts.com

You've
Been
Mugged!

MUG'EMS
by
CQ Products
www.cqproducts.com

Hearty Pasta Soup Mix

1 tsp. dried celery flakes
2 tsp. chopped sun-dried tomatoes
¼ tsp. dried onion flakes
⅛ tsp. garlic powder
2 tsp. beef bouillon
½ tsp. dried oregano
½ tsp. dried basil
2 T. uncooked macaroni or other small pasta
1 (4½ oz.) can chunk chicken, undrained

In small bowl, combine dried celery flakes, chopped sun-dried tomatoes, dried onion flakes, garlic powder, beef bouillon, dried oregano, dried basil and macaroni. Mix well and place in a small ziplock bag and seal. Place can of chicken in mug and top with filled bag. Make sure the mug holds a volume of at least 1½ cups.

Decorate mug and attach a gift tag with the directions on how to prepare the soup.

Gift Tag Directions:
Hearty Pasta Soup

Hearty Pasta Soup Mix
¾ C. water

Preheat oven to 325°. Place Hearty Pasta Soup Mix from bag in mug. In a small saucepan over medium heat, place water. Bring water to a simmer and pour over ingredients in mug. Loosely cover with aluminum foil. Bake in oven for 20 minutes. Remove from oven and stir in chicken in liquid from can. Cover and return to oven for an additional 15 minutes. Enjoy!

Hearty
Pasta Soup

Hearty Pasta Soup Mix
¾ C. water

Preheat oven to 325°. Place Hearty Pasta Soup Mix from bag in mug. In a small saucepan over medium heat, place water. Bring water to a simmer and pour over ingredients in mug. Loosely cover with aluminum foil. Bake in oven for 20 minutes. Remove from oven and stir in chicken in liquid from can. Cover and return to oven for an additional 15 minutes. Enjoy!

Hearty
Pasta Soup

Hearty Pasta Soup Mix
¾ C. water

Preheat oven to 325°. Place Hearty Pasta Soup Mix from bag in mug. In a small saucepan over medium heat, place water. Bring water to a simmer and pour over ingredients in mug. Loosely cover with aluminum foil. Bake in oven for 20 minutes. Remove from oven and stir in chicken in liquid from can. Cover and return to oven for an additional 15 minutes. Enjoy!

You've
Been
Mugged!

MUG'EMS
by
CQ Products
www.cqproducts.com

You've
Been
Mugged!

MUG'EMS
by
CQ Products
www.cqproducts.com

← fold →

Hearty
Pasta Soup

Hearty Pasta Soup Mix
¾ C. water

Preheat oven to 325°. Place Hearty Pasta Soup Mix from bag in mug. In a small saucepan over medium heat, place water. Bring water to a simmer and pour over ingredients in mug. Loosely cover with aluminum foil. Bake in oven for 20 minutes. Remove from oven and stir in chicken in liquid from can. Cover and return to oven for an additional 15 minutes. Enjoy!

Hearty
Pasta Soup

Hearty Pasta Soup Mix
¾ C. water

Preheat oven to 325°. Place Hearty Pasta Soup Mix from bag in mug. In a small saucepan over medium heat, place water. Bring water to a simmer and pour over ingredients in mug. Loosely cover with aluminum foil. Bake in oven for 20 minutes. Remove from oven and stir in chicken in liquid from can. Cover and return to oven for an additional 15 minutes. Enjoy!

fold

You've
Been
Mugged!

You've
Been
Mugged!

MUG'EMS
by
CQ Products
www.cqproducts.com

MUG'EMS
by
CQ Products
www.cqproducts.com

Baked Cheesy Soup Mix

1 T. grated Parmesan cheese
¼ tsp. dried onion flakes
1 tsp. dried celery flakes
2 T. Knorr classic white sauce mix

In a small bowl, combine grated Parmesan cheese, dried onion flakes, dried celery flakes and white sauce mix. Mix well and place in a small ziplock bag and seal. Place sealed bag in a mug. Make sure the mug holds a volume of at least 1½ cups.

Decorate mug and attach a gift tag with the directions on how to prepare the soup.

Gift Tag Directions:
Baked Cheesy Soup

Baked Cheesy Soup Mix
1 C. plus 1 T. milk
1 slice American cheese

Place Baked Cheesy Soup Mix from bag in mug. In small saucepan over medium heat, place milk. Bring milk to a simmer and pour over ingredients in mug. Let sit for 5 minutes. Stir soup and add slice of American cheese. Place mug in microwave for 1 to 2 minutes, until cheese is melted. Mix well. Enjoy!

Baked
Cheesy Soup

Baked Cheesy Soup Mix
1 C. plus 1 T. milk
1 slice American cheese

Place Baked Cheesy Soup Mix from bag in mug. In small saucepan over medium heat, place milk. Bring milk to a simmer and pour over ingredients in mug. Let sit for 5 minutes. Stir soup and add slice of American cheese. Place mug in microwave for 1 to 2 minutes, until cheese is melted. Mix well. Enjoy!

Baked
Cheesy Soup

Baked Cheesy Soup Mix
1 C. plus 1 T. milk
1 slice American cheese

Place Baked Cheesy Soup Mix from bag in mug. In small saucepan over medium heat, place milk. Bring milk to a simmer and pour over ingredients in mug. Let sit for 5 minutes. Stir soup and add slice of American cheese. Place mug in microwave for 1 to 2 minutes, until cheese is melted. Mix well. Enjoy!

fold

You've
Been
Mugged!

You've
Been
Mugged!

MUG'EMS
by
CQ Products
www.cqproducts.com

MUG'EMS
by
CQ Products
www.cqproducts.com

Baked
Cheesy Soup

Baked Cheesy Soup Mix
1 C. plus 1 T. milk
1 slice American cheese

Place Baked Cheesy Soup Mix from bag in mug. In small saucepan over medium heat, place milk. Bring milk to a simmer and pour over ingredients in mug. Let sit for 5 minutes. Stir soup and add slice of American cheese. Place mug in microwave for 1 to 2 minutes, until cheese is melted. Mix well. Enjoy!

Baked
Cheesy Soup

Baked Cheesy Soup Mix
1 C. plus 1 T. milk
1 slice American cheese

Place Baked Cheesy Soup Mix from bag in mug. In small saucepan over medium heat, place milk. Bring milk to a simmer and pour over ingredients in mug. Let sit for 5 minutes. Stir soup and add slice of American cheese. Place mug in microwave for 1 to 2 minutes, until cheese is melted. Mix well. Enjoy!

← fold →

You've
Been
Mugged!

MUG'EMS
by
CQ Products
www.cqproducts.com

You've
Been
Mugged!

MUG'EMS
by
CQ Products
www.cqproducts.com

Tomato Soup Mix

2 tsp. beef bouillon
½ tsp. dried onion flakes
1 tsp. dried celery flakes
½ tsp. crumbled bay leaf
1½ T. powdered coffee creamer

In small bowl, combine beef bouillon, dried onion flakes, dried celery flakes, crumbled bay leaf and powdered coffee creamer. Mix well and place in a small ziplock bag and seal. Place sealed bag in a mug. Make sure the mug holds a volume of at least 1½ cups.

Decorate mug and attach a gift tag with the directions on how to prepare the soup.

Gift Tag Directions:
Tomato Soup

Tomato Soup Mix
1 C. water
2½ T. tomato paste
½ T. butter

Place Tomato Soup Mix from bag in mug. In small saucepan over medium heat, place water. Bring water to a boil and pour over ingredients in mug. Stir slightly and add tomato paste and butter, stirring until well incorporated. Let sit for 5 minutes. Place mug in microwave for 1 minute, heating until soup is simmering. Enjoy!

Tomato Soup

Tomato Soup Mix
1 C. water
2½ T. tomato paste
½ T. butter

Place Tomato Soup Mix from bag in mug. In small saucepan over medium heat, place water. Bring water to a boil and pour over ingredients in mug. Stir slightly and add tomato paste and butter, stirring until well incorporated. Let sit for 5 minutes. Place mug in microwave for 1 minute, heating until soup is simmering. Enjoy!

Tomato Soup

Tomato Soup Mix
1 C. water
2½ T. tomato paste
½ T. butter

Place Tomato Soup Mix from bag in mug. In small saucepan over medium heat, place water. Bring water to a boil and pour over ingredients in mug. Stir slightly and add tomato paste and butter, stirring until well incorporated. Let sit for 5 minutes. Place mug in microwave for 1 minute, heating until soup is simmering. Enjoy!

You've
Been
Mugged!

MUG'EMS
by
CQ Products
www.cqproducts.com

You've
Been
Mugged!

MUG'EMS
by
CQ Products
www.cqproducts.com

← fold →

Tomato Soup

Tomato Soup Mix
1 C. water
2½ T. tomato paste
½ T. butter

Place Tomato Soup Mix from bag in mug. In small saucepan over medium heat, place water. Bring water to a boil and pour over ingredients in mug. Stir slightly and add tomato paste and butter, stirring until well incorporated. Let sit for 5 minutes. Place mug in microwave for 1 minute, heating until soup is simmering. Enjoy!

Tomato Soup

Tomato Soup Mix
1 C. water
2½ T. tomato paste
½ T. butter

Place Tomato Soup Mix from bag in mug. In small saucepan over medium heat, place water. Bring water to a boil and pour over ingredients in mug. Stir slightly and add tomato paste and butter, stirring until well incorporated. Let sit for 5 minutes. Place mug in microwave for 1 minute, heating until soup is simmering. Enjoy!

← fold →

You've
Been
Mugged!

You've
Been
Mugged!

MUG'EMS
by
CQ Products
www.cqproducts.com

MUG'EMS
by
CQ Products
www.cqproducts.com

Bran Nut Bread Mix

3 T. bran flakes
4 T. whole wheat flour
1 T. brown sugar
¾ tsp. baking powder
⅛ tsp. salt
1 T. raisins
Pinch of nutmeg
1/4 tsp. cinnamon
1 T. chopped walnuts or pecans

In a small bowl, combine bran flakes, whole wheat flour, brown sugar, baking powder, salt, raisins, nutmeg, cinnamon and chopped walnuts. Mix well and place in a small ziplock bag and seal. Place sealed bag in a mug. Make sure the mug holds a volume of at least 1½ cups.

Decorate mug and attach a gift tag with the directions on how to prepare the bread.

Gift Tag Directions:
Bran Nut Bread

Bran Nut Bread Mix
1 T. vegetable oil
2 T. buttermilk
1 egg, beaten

Preheat oven to 350°. In a small mixing bowl, combine Bran Nut Bread Mix from bag with vegetable oil, buttermilk and half of the beaten egg. Mix well and pour into lightly greased mug. Bake in oven for 20 to 25 minutes. Enjoy!

Bran Nut Bread

Bran Nut Bread Mix
1 T. vegetable oil
2 T. buttermilk
1 egg, beaten

Preheat oven to 350°. In a small mixing bowl, combine Bran Nut Bread Mix from bag with vegetable oil, buttermilk and half of the beaten egg. Mix well and pour into lightly greased mug. Bake in oven for 20 to 25 minutes. Enjoy!

Bran Nut Bread

Bran Nut Bread Mix
1 T. vegetable oil
2 T. buttermilk
1 egg, beaten

Preheat oven to 350°. In a small mixing bowl, combine Bran Nut Bread Mix from bag with vegetable oil, buttermilk and half of the beaten egg. Mix well and pour into lightly greased mug. Bake in oven for 20 to 25 minutes. Enjoy!

You've
Been
Mugged!

MUG'EMS
by
CQ Products
www.cqproducts.com

You've
Been
Mugged!

MUG'EMS
by
CQ Products
www.cqproducts.com

Bran Nut Bread

Bran Nut Bread Mix
1 T. vegetable oil
2 T. buttermilk
1 egg, beaten

Preheat oven to 350°. In a small mixing bowl, combine Bran Nut Bread Mix from bag with vegetable oil, buttermilk and half of the beaten egg. Mix well and pour into lightly greased mug. Bake in oven for 20 to 25 minutes. Enjoy!

Bran Nut Bread

Bran Nut Bread Mix
1 T. vegetable oil
2 T. buttermilk
1 egg, beaten

Preheat oven to 350°. In a small mixing bowl, combine Bran Nut Bread Mix from bag with vegetable oil, buttermilk and half of the beaten egg. Mix well and pour into lightly greased mug. Bake in oven for 20 to 25 minutes. Enjoy!

fold

You've Been Mugged!

You've Been Mugged!

MUG'EMS
by
CQ Products
www.cqproducts.com

MUG'EMS
by
CQ Products
www.cqproducts.com

Banana Bread Mix

1 T. finely chopped walnuts
⅓ C. flour
½ tsp. baking powder
¼ tsp. baking soda
1½ T. sugar

In a small bowl, combine chopped walnuts, flour, baking powder, baking soda and sugar. Mix well and place in small ziplock bag and seal. Place sealed bag in a mug. Make sure the mug holds a volume of at least 1½ cups.

Decorate mug and attach a gift tag with the directions on how to prepare the bread.

Gift Tag Directions:
Banana Bread

Banana Bread Mix
2 T. margarine or shortening
½ tsp. vanilla
2 T. mashed banana
1 egg yolk
1½ T. sour cream

Preheat oven to 350°. In small mixing bowl, place Banana Bread Mix from bag. Using a pastry blender, cut in margarine until mixture resembles fine crumbs. Add vanilla, mashed banana, egg yolk and sour cream. Stir until well combined and pour batter into lightly greased mug. Bake in oven for 20 to 25 minutes. Enjoy!

Banana Bread

Banana Bread Mix
2 T. margarine or shortening
½ tsp. vanilla
2 T. mashed banana
1 egg yolk
1½ T. sour cream

   Preheat oven to 350°. In small mixing bowl, place Banana Bread Mix from bag. Using a pastry blender, cut in margarine until mixture resembles fine crumbs. Add vanilla, mashed banana, egg yolk and sour cream. Stir until well combined and pour batter into lightly greased mug. Bake in oven for 20 to 25 minutes. Enjoy!

Banana Bread

Banana Bread Mix
2 T. margarine or shortening
½ tsp. vanilla
2 T. mashed banana
1 egg yolk
1½ T. sour cream

   Preheat oven to 350°. In small mixing bowl, place Banana Bread Mix from bag. Using a pastry blender, cut in margarine until mixture resembles fine crumbs. Add vanilla, mashed banana, egg yolk and sour cream. Stir until well combined and pour batter into lightly greased mug. Bake in oven for 20 to 25 minutes. Enjoy!

You've
Been
Mugged!

MUG'EMS
by
CQ Products
www.cqproducts.com

You've
Been
Mugged!

MUG'EMS
by
CQ Products
www.cqproducts.com

← fold →

Banana Bread

Banana Bread Mix
2 T. margarine or shortening
½ tsp. vanilla
2 T. mashed banana
1 egg yolk
1½ T. sour cream

Preheat oven to 350°. In small mixing bowl, place Banana Bread Mix from bag. Using a pastry blender, cut in margarine until mixture resembles fine crumbs. Add vanilla, mashed banana, egg yolk and sour cream. Stir until well combined and pour batter into lightly greased mug. Bake in oven for 20 to 25 minutes. Enjoy!

Banana Bread

Banana Bread Mix
2 T. margarine or shortening
½ tsp. vanilla
2 T. mashed banana
1 egg yolk
1½ T. sour cream

Preheat oven to 350°. In small mixing bowl, place Banana Bread Mix from bag. Using a pastry blender, cut in margarine until mixture resembles fine crumbs. Add vanilla, mashed banana, egg yolk and sour cream. Stir until well combined and pour batter into lightly greased mug. Bake in oven for 20 to 25 minutes. Enjoy!

fold

You've
Been
Mugged!

MUG'EMS
by
CQ Products
www.cqproducts.com

You've
Been
Mugged!

MUG'EMS
by
CQ Products
www.cqproducts.com

Pecan Brown Bread Mix

3 T. whole wheat flour
2 T. cornmeal
2 T. flour
¼ tsp. baking powder
¼ tsp. baking soda
2 T. raisins
1 T. finely chopped pecans

In a small bowl, combine whole wheat flour, cornmeal, flour, baking powder, baking soda, raisins and chopped pecans. Mix well and place in a small ziplock bag and seal. Place sealed bag in a mug. Make sure the mug holds a volume of at least 1½ cups.

Decorate mug and attach a gift tag with the directions on how to prepare the bread.

Gift Tag Directions:
Pecan Brown Bread

Pecan Brown Bread Mix
1 T. molasses
2 T. buttermilk
1 egg

Preheat oven to 325°. In a small mixing bowl, combine Pecan Brown Bread Mix from bag with molasses, buttermilk and egg. Mix well and pour batter into lightly greased mug. Place mug in a pot. Fill pot with water until water level is halfway up side of mug. Place pot with mug in oven and bake for 30 to 35 minutes. Enjoy!

Pecan
Brown Bread

Pecan Brown Bread Mix
1 T. molasses
2 T. buttermilk
1 egg

Preheat oven to 325°. In a small mixing bowl, combine Pecan Brown Bread Mix from bag with molasses, buttermilk and egg. Mix well and pour batter into lightly greased mug. Place mug in a pot. Fill pot with water until water level is halfway up side of mug. Place pot with mug in oven and bake for 30 to 35 minutes. Enjoy!

Pecan
Brown Bread

Pecan Brown Bread Mix
1 T. molasses
2 T. buttermilk
1 egg

Preheat oven to 325°. In a small mixing bowl, combine Pecan Brown Bread Mix from bag with molasses, buttermilk and egg. Mix well and pour batter into lightly greased mug. Place mug in a pot. Fill pot with water until water level is halfway up side of mug. Place pot with mug in oven and bake for 30 to 35 minutes. Enjoy!

← fold →

You've
Been
Mugged!

You've
Been
Mugged!

MUG'EMS
by
CQ Products
www.cqproducts.com

MUG'EMS
by
CQ Products
www.cqproducts.com

Pecan
Brown Bread

Pecan Brown Bread Mix
1 T. molasses
2 T. buttermilk
1 egg

Preheat oven to 325°. In a small mixing bowl, combine Pecan Brown Bread Mix from bag with molasses, buttermilk and egg. Mix well and pour batter into lightly greased mug. Place mug in a pot. Fill pot with water until water level is halfway up side of mug. Place pot with mug in oven and bake for 30 to 35 minutes. Enjoy!

Pecan
Brown Bread

Pecan Brown Bread Mix
1 T. molasses
2 T. buttermilk
1 egg

Preheat oven to 325°. In a small mixing bowl, combine Pecan Brown Bread Mix from bag with molasses, buttermilk and egg. Mix well and pour batter into lightly greased mug. Place mug in a pot. Fill pot with water until water level is halfway up side of mug. Place pot with mug in oven and bake for 30 to 35 minutes. Enjoy!

← fold →

You've
Been
Mugged!

You've
Been
Mugged!

MUG'EMS
by
CQ Products
www.cqproducts.com

MUG'EMS
by
CQ Products
www.cqproducts.com

French Onion Soup Mix

1 tsp. beef bouillon
1 T. brown gravy mix
1 tsp. dried onion flakes
¾ tsp. sugar
1 tsp. chopped sun-dried tomatoes
½ tsp. dried parsley flakes
¼ C. dried, cubed bread

In a small bowl, combine beef bouillon, brown gravy mix, dried onion flakes, sugar, chopped sun-dried tomatoes and dried parsley flakes. Mix well and place in a small ziplock bag and seal. Place sealed bag in a mug. Make sure the mug holds a volume of at least 1½ cups. In a separate ziplock bag, place dried, cubed bread. Place bag in mug with other bag.

Decorate mug and attach a gift tag with the directions on how to prepare the soup.

Gift Tag Directions:
French Onion Soup

French Onion Soup Mix
1 C. water
2 T. shredded mozzarella cheese

Preheat oven to 400°. Place contents of bag containing sun-dried tomatoes in mug. In a small saucepan, place water. Bring water to a boil and pour over ingredients in mug. Let mixture sit for 5 minutes. Top soup with bread crumbs from remaining bag and shredded mozzarella cheese. Bake in oven for 6 to 10 minutes, until cheese is melted. Or, if desired, mug can be placed under broiler for 4 to 5 minutes, until cheese is bubbly and begins to brown. Enjoy!

French Onion Soup

French Onion Soup Mix
1 C. water
2 T. shredded mozzarella cheese

Preheat oven to 400°. Place contents of bag containing sun-dried tomatoes in mug. In a small saucepan, place water. Bring water to a boil and pour over ingredients in mug. Let mixture sit for 5 minutes. Top soup with bread crumbs from remaining bag and shredded mozzarella cheese. Bake in oven for 6 to 10 minutes, until cheese is melted. Or, if desired, mug can be placed under broiler for 4 to 5 minutes, until cheese is bubbly and begins to brown. Enjoy!

French Onion Soup

French Onion Soup Mix
1 C. water
2 T. shredded mozzarella cheese

Preheat oven to 400°. Place contents of bag containing sun-dried tomatoes in mug. In a small saucepan, place water. Bring water to a boil and pour over ingredients in mug. Let mixture sit for 5 minutes. Top soup with bread crumbs from remaining bag and shredded mozzarella cheese. Bake in oven for 6 to 10 minutes, until cheese is melted. Or, if desired, mug can be placed under broiler for 4 to 5 minutes, until cheese is bubbly and begins to brown. Enjoy!

fold

You've
Been
Mugged!

You've
Been
Mugged!

MUG'EMS
by
CQ Products
www.cqproducts.com

MUG'EMS
by
CQ Products
www.cqproducts.com

French Onion Soup

French Onion Soup Mix
1 C. water
2 T. shredded mozzarella
cheese

Preheat oven to 400°. Place contents of bag containing sun-dried tomatoes in mug. In a small saucepan, place water. Bring water to a boil and pour over ingredients in mug. Let mixture sit for 5 minutes. Top soup with bread crumbs from remaining bag and shredded mozzarella cheese. Bake in oven for 6 to 10 minutes, until cheese is melted. Or, if desired, mug can be placed under broiler for 4 to 5 minutes, until cheese is bubbly and begins to brown. Enjoy!

French Onion Soup

French Onion Soup Mix
1 C. water
2 T. shredded mozzarella
cheese

Preheat oven to 400°. Place contents of bag containing sun-dried tomatoes in mug. In a small saucepan, place water. Bring water to a boil and pour over ingredients in mug. Let mixture sit for 5 minutes. Top soup with bread crumbs from remaining bag and shredded mozzarella cheese. Bake in oven for 6 to 10 minutes, until cheese is melted. Or, if desired, mug can be placed under broiler for 4 to 5 minutes, until cheese is bubbly and begins to brown. Enjoy!

fold

You've
Been
Mugged!

You've
Been
Mugged!

MUG'EMS
by
CQ Products
www.cqproducts.com

MUG'EMS
by
CQ Products
www.cqproducts.com

Southwestern Beef Stew Mix

2 T. dried hash brown potatoes
1 tsp. chopped sun-dried tomatoes
1 T. brown gravy mix
1 tsp. beef bouillon
¼ tsp. dried onion flakes
1 tsp. dried celery flakes
⅛ tsp. garlic powder
⅛ tsp. pepper
1 tsp. dried bell pepper

In a small bowl, combine dried hash brown potatoes, chopped sun-dried tomatoes, brown gravy mix, beef bouillon, dried onion flakes, dried celery flakes, garlic powder. Mix well and place in a small ziplock bag and seal. Place sealed bag in a mug. Make sure the mug holds a volume of at least 1½ cups.

Decorate mug and attach a gift tag with the directions on how to prepare the stew.

Gift Tag Directions:
Southwestern Beef Stew

Southwestern Beef Stew Mix
1 C. water
¼ C. to ⅓ C. ground beef

Place Southwestern Beef Stew Mix from bag in mug. In a small saucepan over medium heat, place water. Bring to a boil and pour over ingredients in mug. Let sit for 5 to 10 minutes. Meanwhile, in a small skillet over medium heat, brown ground beef and drain of fat. Add browned beef to ingredients in mug and heat in microwave for 1 minute. Enjoy!

Southwestern Beef Stew

Southwestern Beef Stew Mix
1 C. water
¼ C. to ⅓ C. ground beef

Place Southwestern Beef Stew Mix from bag in mug. In a small saucepan over medium heat, place water. Bring to a boil and pour over ingredients in mug. Let sit for 5 to 10 minutes. Meanwhile, in a small skillet over medium heat, brown ground beef and drain of fat. Add browned beef to ingredients in mug and heat in microwave for 1 minute. Enjoy!

Southwestern Beef Stew

Southwestern Beef Stew Mix
1 C. water
¼ C. to ⅓ C. ground beef

Place Southwestern Beef Stew Mix from bag in mug. In a small saucepan over medium heat, place water. Bring to a boil and pour over ingredients in mug. Let sit for 5 to 10 minutes. Meanwhile, in a small skillet over medium heat, brown ground beef and drain of fat. Add browned beef to ingredients in mug and heat in microwave for 1 minute. Enjoy!

← fold →

You've
Been
Mugged!

MUG'EMS
by
CQ Products
www.cqproducts.com

You've
Been
Mugged!

MUG'EMS
by
CQ Products
www.cqproducts.com

Southwestern Beef Stew

Southwestern Beef Stew Mix
1 C. water
¼ C. to ⅓ C. ground beef

Place Southwestern Beef Stew Mix from bag in mug. In a small saucepan over medium heat, place water. Bring to a boil and pour over ingredients in mug. Let sit for 5 to 10 minutes. Meanwhile, in a small skillet over medium heat, brown ground beef and drain of fat. Add browned beef to ingredients in mug and heat in microwave for 1 minute. Enjoy!

Southwestern Beef Stew

Southwestern Beef Stew Mix
1 C. water
¼ C. to ⅓ C. ground beef

Place Southwestern Beef Stew Mix from bag in mug. In a small saucepan over medium heat, place water. Bring to a boil and pour over ingredients in mug. Let sit for 5 to 10 minutes. Meanwhile, in a small skillet over medium heat, brown ground beef and drain of fat. Add browned beef to ingredients in mug and heat in microwave for 1 minute. Enjoy!

fold

You've
Been
Mugged!

You've
Been
Mugged!

MUG'EMS
by
CQ Products
www.cqproducts.com

MUG'EMS
by
CQ Products
www.cqproducts.com

Tortilla Soup Mix

4 T. crushed tortilla chips
1 T. instant rice
1 tsp. chicken bouillon
¼ tsp. dried onion flakes
Pinch of garlic powder
⅛ tsp. chili powder
Pinch of salt
1 (4½ oz.) can chunk chicken, drained

In a small bowl, combine crushed tortilla chips, instant rice, chicken bouillon, dried onion flakes, garlic powder, chili powder and salt. Mix well and place in a small ziplock bag and seal. Place can of chicken in mug and top with filled bag. Make sure the mug holds a volume of at least 1½ cups.

Decorate mug and attach a gift tag with the directions on how to prepare the soup.

Gift Tag Directions:
Tortilla Soup

Tortilla Soup Mix
¾ C. water

Place Tortilla Soup Mix from bag in mug. In a small saucepan over medium heat, place water. Bring water to a simmer and pour over ingredients in mug. Let mixture sit for 5 minutes. Add drained chicken from can to ingredients in mug. Mix well and heat in microwave for 2 minutes. If desired, top with shredded Cheddar cheese, salsa or sour cream. Enjoy!

Tortilla Soup

Tortilla Soup Mix
¾ C. water

Place Tortilla Soup Mix from bag in mug. In a small saucepan over medium heat, place water. Bring water to a simmer and pour over ingredients in mug. Let mixture sit for 5 minutes. Add drained chicken from can to ingredients in mug. Mix well and heat in microwave for 2 minutes. If desired, top with shredded Cheddar cheese, salsa or sour cream. Enjoy!

Tortilla Soup

Tortilla Soup Mix
¾ C. water

Place Tortilla Soup Mix from bag in mug. In a small saucepan over medium heat, place water. Bring water to a simmer and pour over ingredients in mug. Let mixture sit for 5 minutes. Add drained chicken from can to ingredients in mug. Mix well and heat in microwave for 2 minutes. If desired, top with shredded Cheddar cheese, salsa or sour cream. Enjoy!

← fold →

You've
Been
Mugged!

You've
Been
Mugged!

MUG'EMS
by
CQ Products
www.cqproducts.com

MUG'EMS
by
CQ Products
www.cqproducts.com

Tortilla Soup

Tortilla Soup Mix
¾ C. water

Place Tortilla Soup Mix from bag in mug. In a small saucepan over medium heat, place water. Bring water to a simmer and pour over ingredients in mug. Let mixture sit for 5 minutes. Add drained chicken from can to ingredients in mug. Mix well and heat in microwave for 2 minutes. If desired, top with shredded Cheddar cheese, salsa or sour cream. Enjoy!

Tortilla Soup

Tortilla Soup Mix
¾ C. water

Place Tortilla Soup Mix from bag in mug. In a small saucepan over medium heat, place water. Bring water to a simmer and pour over ingredients in mug. Let mixture sit for 5 minutes. Add drained chicken from can to ingredients in mug. Mix well and heat in microwave for 2 minutes. If desired, top with shredded Cheddar cheese, salsa or sour cream. Enjoy!

← fold →

You've
Been
Mugged!

You've
Been
Mugged!

MUG'EMS
by
CQ Products
www.cqproducts.com

MUG'EMS
by
CQ Products
www.cqproducts.com

Apple Spice Bread Mix

⅓ C. flour
¾ tsp. baking powder
2 T. dried chopped apples
Pinch of salt
¼ tsp. cinnamon
Pinch of nutmeg
Pinch of ground cloves
1½ T. brown sugar

In a small bowl, combine flour, baking powder, dried chopped apples, salt, cinnamon, nutmeg, ground cloves and brown sugar. Mix well and place in small ziplock bag and seal. Place sealed bag in a mug. Make sure the mug holds a volume of at least 1½ cups.

Decorate mug and attach a gift tag with the directions on how to prepare the bread.

Gift Tag Directions:
Apple Spice Bread

Apple Spice Bread Mix
3 T. milk
1 T. butter
1 egg, beaten

Preheat oven to 350°. Place Apple Spice Bread Mix from bag in a small mixing bowl. In a small saucepan over medium heat, combine milk and butter. Heat until butter is melted. Add half of the beaten egg and heated milk mixture to ingredients in bowl. Mix well and pour batter into lightly greased mug. Bake in oven for 20 to 25 minutes. Enjoy!

Apple Spice Bread

Apple Spice Bread Mix
3 T. milk
1 T. butter
1 egg, beaten

Preheat oven to 350°. Place Apple Spice Bread Mix from bag in a small mixing bowl. In a small saucepan over medium heat, combine milk and butter. Heat until butter is melted. Add half of the beaten egg and heated milk mixture to ingredients in bowl. Mix well and pour batter into lightly greased mug. Bake in oven for 20 to 25 minutes. Enjoy!

Apple Spice Bread

Apple Spice Bread Mix
3 T. milk
1 T. butter
1 egg, beaten

Preheat oven to 350°. Place Apple Spice Bread Mix from bag in a small mixing bowl. In a small saucepan over medium heat, combine milk and butter. Heat until butter is melted. Add half of the beaten egg and heated milk mixture to ingredients in bowl. Mix well and pour batter into lightly greased mug. Bake in oven for 20 to 25 minutes. Enjoy!

You've
Been
Mugged!

MUG'EMS
by
CQ Products
www.cqproducts.com

You've
Been
Mugged!

MUG'EMS
by
CQ Products
www.cqproducts.com

← fold →

Apple Spice Bread

Apple Spice Bread Mix
3 T. milk
1 T. butter
1 egg, beaten

Preheat oven to 350°. Place Apple Spice Bread Mix from bag in a small mixing bowl. In a small saucepan over medium heat, combine milk and butter. Heat until butter is melted. Add half of the beaten egg and heated milk mixture to ingredients in bowl. Mix well and pour batter into lightly greased mug. Bake in oven for 20 to 25 minutes. Enjoy!

Apple Spice Bread

Apple Spice Bread Mix
3 T. milk
1 T. butter
1 egg, beaten

Preheat oven to 350°. Place Apple Spice Bread Mix from bag in a small mixing bowl. In a small saucepan over medium heat, combine milk and butter. Heat until butter is melted. Add half of the beaten egg and heated milk mixture to ingredients in bowl. Mix well and pour batter into lightly greased mug. Bake in oven for 20 to 25 minutes. Enjoy!

← fold →

You've
Been
Mugged!

You've
Been
Mugged!

MUG'EMS
by
CQ Products
www.cqproducts.com

MUG'EMS
by
CQ Products
www.cqproducts.com

Graham Cracker Bread Mix

1 T. sugar
1 T. dark brown sugar
3 T. graham cracker crumbs
¼ C. flour
½ tsp. baking powder
¼ tsp. baking soda
2 tsp. golden raisins

In a small bowl, combine sugar, brown sugar, graham cracker crumbs, flour, baking powder, baking soda and raisins. Mix well and place in small ziplock bag and seal. Place sealed bag in a mug. Make sure the mug holds a volume of at least 1½ cups.

Decorate mug and attach a gift tag with the directions on how to prepare the bread.

Gift tag directions:
Graham Cracker Bread

Graham Cracker Bread Mix
1 egg, beaten
½ T. vegetable oil
3 T. buttermilk or 2 T. milk

Preheat oven to 350°. In a small bowl, place Graham Cracker Bread Mix from bag. Add half of the beaten egg, vegetable oil and buttermilk. Mix until well incorporated and pour batter into lightly greased mug. Bake in oven for 16 to 20 minutes. Enjoy!

Graham Cracker Bread

Graham Cracker Bread Mix
1 egg, beaten
½ T. vegetable oil
3 T. buttermilk or 2 T. milk

Preheat oven to 350°. In a small bowl, place Graham Cracker Bread Mix from bag. Add half of the beaten egg, vegetable oil and buttermilk. Mix until well incorporated and pour batter into lightly greased mug. Bake in oven for 16 to 20 minutes. Enjoy!

Graham Cracker Bread

Graham Cracker Bread Mix
1 egg, beaten
½ T. vegetable oil
3 T. buttermilk or 2 T. milk

Preheat oven to 350°. In a small bowl, place Graham Cracker Bread Mix from bag. Add half of the beaten egg, vegetable oil and buttermilk. Mix until well incorporated and pour batter into lightly greased mug. Bake in oven for 16 to 20 minutes. Enjoy!

fold

You've
Been
Mugged!

You've
Been
Mugged!

MUG'EMS
by
CQ Products
www.cqproducts.com

MUG'EMS
by
CQ Products
www.cqproducts.com

Graham Cracker Bread

Graham Cracker Bread Mix
1 egg, beaten
½ T. vegetable oil
3 T. buttermilk or 2 T. milk

Preheat oven to 350°. In a small bowl, place Graham Cracker Bread Mix from bag. Add half of the beaten egg, vegetable oil and buttermilk. Mix until well incorporated and pour batter into lightly greased mug. Bake in oven for 16 to 20 minutes. Enjoy!

Graham Cracker Bread

Graham Cracker Bread Mix
1 egg, beaten
½ T. vegetable oil
3 T. buttermilk or 2 T. milk

Preheat oven to 350°. In a small bowl, place Graham Cracker Bread Mix from bag. Add half of the beaten egg, vegetable oil and buttermilk. Mix until well incorporated and pour batter into lightly greased mug. Bake in oven for 16 to 20 minutes. Enjoy!

← fold →

You've
Been
Mugged!

You've
Been
Mugged!

MUG'EMS
by
CQ Products
www.cqproducts.com

MUG'EMS
by
CQ Products
www.cqproducts.com

Chicken Tomato Stew Mix

2 T. instant rice
2½ T. brown gravy mix
1 tsp. chicken bouillon
1 tsp. dried parsley flakes
¼ tsp. dried onion flakes
⅛ tsp. dried minced garlic
1 tsp. dried celery flakes
1 tsp. chopped sun-dried tomatoes
1 (4½ oz.) can chunk chicken, drained

In a small bowl, combine instant rice, brown gravy mix, chicken bouillon, dried parsley flakes, dried onion flakes, dried minced garlic, dried celery flakes and chopped sun-dried tomatoes. Mix well and place in a small ziplock bag and seal. Place can of chicken in mug and top with filled bag. Make sure the mug holds a volume of at least 1½ cups.

Decorate mug and attach a gift tag with the directions on how to prepare stew.

Gift Tag Directions:
Chicken Tomato Stew

Chicken Tomato Stew Mix
¾ C. water

Place Chicken Tomato Stew Mix from bag in mug. In a small saucepan over medium heat, place water. Bring to a boil and pour over ingredients in mug. Cover and let mixture sit for 5 minutes. Add drained chicken from can and mix until well incorporated. Heat in microwave for 2 minutes. Enjoy!

Chicken
Tomato Stew

Chicken Tomato Stew Mix
¾ C. water

Place Chicken Tomato Stew Mix from bag in mug. In a small saucepan over medium heat, place water. Bring to a boil and pour over ingredients in mug. Cover and let mixture sit for 5 minutes. Add drained chicken from can and mix until well incorporated. Heat in microwave for 2 minutes. Enjoy!

Chicken
Tomato Stew

Chicken Tomato Stew Mix
¾ C. water

Place Chicken Tomato Stew Mix from bag in mug. In a small saucepan over medium heat, place water. Bring to a boil and pour over ingredients in mug. Cover and let mixture sit for 5 minutes. Add drained chicken from can and mix until well incorporated. Heat in microwave for 2 minutes. Enjoy!

← fold →

You've
Been
Mugged!

MUG'EMS
by
CQ Products
www.cqproducts.com

You've
Been
Mugged!

MUG'EMS
by
CQ Products
www.cqproducts.com

Chicken
Tomato Stew

Chicken Tomato Stew Mix
¾ C. water

Place Chicken Tomato Stew Mix from bag in mug. In a small saucepan over medium heat, place water. Bring to a boil and pour over ingredients in mug. Cover and let mixture sit for 5 minutes. Add drained chicken from can and mix until well incorporated. Heat in microwave for 2 minutes. Enjoy!

Chicken
Tomato Stew

Chicken Tomato Stew Mix
¾ C. water

Place Chicken Tomato Stew Mix from bag in mug. In a small saucepan over medium heat, place water. Bring to a boil and pour over ingredients in mug. Cover and let mixture sit for 5 minutes. Add drained chicken from can and mix until well incorporated. Heat in microwave for 2 minutes. Enjoy!

You've
Been
Mugged!

MUG'EMS
by
CQ Products
www.cqproducts.com

You've
Been
Mugged!

MUG'EMS
by
CQ Products
www.cqproducts.com

fold

Cream of Celery Soup Mix

2 T. Knorr classic white sauce mix
1 T. dried celery flakes
¼ tsp. celery salt
1 tsp. chicken bouillon
⅛ tsp. pepper

In a small bowl, combine white sauce mix, dried celery flakes, celery salt, chicken bouillon and pepper. Mix well and place in small ziplock bag and seal. Place sealed bag in a mug. Make sure the mug holds a volume of at least 1½ cups.

Decorate mug and attach a gift tag with the directions on how to prepare the soup.

Gift Tag Directions:
Cream of Celery Soup

Cream of Celery Soup Mix
1 C. milk

Place Cream of Celery Soup Mix from bag in mug. Add milk and stir until well incorporated. Heat in microwave for 2 minutes. Stir and return to microwave for an additional 1 to 2 minutes, until heated throughout. Enjoy!

Cream of
Celery Soup

Cream of Celery Soup Mix
1 C. milk

Place Cream of Celery Soup
Mix from bag in mug. Add milk and
stir until well incorporated. Heat
in microwave for 2 minutes. Stir
and return to microwave for an
additional 1 to 2 minutes, until
heated throughout. Enjoy!

Cream of
Celery Soup

Cream of Celery Soup Mix
1 C. milk

Place Cream of Celery Soup
Mix from bag in mug. Add milk and
stir until well incorporated. Heat
in microwave for 2 minutes. Stir
and return to microwave for an
additional 1 to 2 minutes, until
heated throughout. Enjoy!

You've
Been
Mugged!

MUG'EMS
by
CQ Products
www.cqproducts.com

You've
Been
Mugged!

MUG'EMS
by
CQ Products
www.cqproducts.com

← fold →

Cream of
Celery Soup

Cream of Celery Soup Mix
1 C. milk

Place Cream of Celery Soup Mix from bag in mug. Add milk and stir until well incorporated. Heat in microwave for 2 minutes. Stir and return to microwave for an additional 1 to 2 minutes, until heated throughout. Enjoy!

Cream of
Celery Soup

Cream of Celery Soup Mix
1 C. milk

Place Cream of Celery Soup Mix from bag in mug. Add milk and stir until well incorporated. Heat in microwave for 2 minutes. Stir and return to microwave for an additional 1 to 2 minutes, until heated throughout. Enjoy!

fold

You've
Been
Mugged!

You've
Been
Mugged!

MUG'EMS.
by
CQ Products
www.cqproducts.com

MUG'EMS
by
CQ Products
www.cqproducts.com

Index

Tips on Preparing & Decorating:

- Holiday themed food-safe bags, normally found at your local craft store, add a nice touch to your gift.

- It is often easier to place the open bag in the mug first. Then pour the ingredients into the open bag and seal. If needed, use a thin paper plate as a funnel.

- Before decorating the bag with ribbon, raffia or a fabric strip, first close the bag with a rubber band or twist tie.

- Add your personalized greeting to one side of the gift tag then fold in half. Punch a hole into the corner of the tag and use ribbon, raffia, twine, lace or a fabric strip to attach the tag to the mug.

- Mug 'Ems make great gifts for Mother's Day, birthdays, holidays or a sick friend. Accessorize the gift by attaching a small gift such as a stirring spoon, fork or hot pad to the mug.